Making Church More Enjoyable

David R. Mains

David C. Cook Publishing Co.

ELGIN, ILLINOIS—WESTON, ONTARIO

MAKING CHURCH MORE ENJOYABLE
© 1980 David R. Mains

All Scripture quotations are from the Revised Standard Version unless otherwise noted.

Published by David C. Cook Publishing Co., Elgin, IL 60120
Cover design by Joe Ragont
Printed in the United States of America
ISBN 0-89191-256-8
LC 80-51274

CONTENTS

The Chapel Talks Series by David Mains

Making Church More Enjoyable
How to Support Your Pastor
How to Resist Temptation
God, Help Us with the Kids
What's Wrong with Lukewarm?
Praying More Effectively
Getting to Know the Holy Spirit
When God Gets Angry with a Nation
A Closer Walk with God
Psalms That Touch Us Where We Live
Making Scripture Yours
I Needed That Encouragement

INTRODUCTION

Most people listen to the radio while they're doing something else. As a broadcaster I'm aware that a person hearing me is probably shaving, fixing breakfast, driving to work, or some similar activity. Being able to keep his or her attention in such a setting is a lot different than preaching to a captive audience.

Therefore, I was dubious as to whether the slow pace of radio with its need for frequent repetition and underscoring each key truth would transfer all that well into print.

To complicate matters further, every time a program is made I must assume many listeners didn't hear what was said the day before. But just the opposite is true when compiling the chapters of a book. They build on one another.

Well, the first series of Chapel talks is now completed. Through the help of others, my broadcast scripts have been made more readable than I thought possible. The greatest thanks for this project goes to my wife, Karen, who put aside her own writing to help me out. Two Chapel of the Air staff members, Ruby Christian and Sharon Morse, also did yeoman duty typing long hours after work and on weekends.

1

PLEASING GOD WITH OUR WORSHIP

What did you talk about in the car on the way to church this last Sunday morning? I know that a lot has happened since then, but maybe a couple of questions could jog your memory. (Some of you live so close to your place of worship there's hardly time to strike up a conversation. You should attempt to reconstruct what transpired at home the hour before you left. Or if you didn't make it to church this past Sunday, think about the last time you went.)

In looking back, was getting ready for church a pleasant time? It's peculiar, isn't it, how so often somebody in a family is unhappy on the Lord's Day! In fact, I have it on good authority that certain people never get upset *except* on Sunday morning before church! Did you have time to read your paper before you left? Did you listen to the car radio as you drove? Somewhere during the whole process, was there time to pray, or were you simply too rushed?

The key questions I want to pose are these: Do you recall preparing yourself in any way to honor God in the upcoming worship service? Was anything of a spiritual nature discussed with the family to get them ready to attend church?

Then what about the trip home? What did you talk about? Spiritual matters? If you commented on the hour spent in God's house, was the tone of your remarks positive or negative? Would you say the general nature of your conversation was self-centered or God-centered? Did you get past personal feelings on matters and attempt to see the services from the Lord's eyes?

For example, do you think God was pleased with the sermon because it truly represented his thoughts? Was it a day when you, along with God's people, outdid yourselves in expressing your appreciation of him. Or did he have to put up with a "business-as-usual" procedure?

Most Christians have a tendency to be selfish in their attitudes toward worship. Too often they judge Sunday mornings solely on the basis of what *they* got out of it. Yet it is possible that the choral selection, which was meaningless to you, was extremely satisfying to God, because it was an anthem of pure praise addressed to our Heavenly Father regarding his everlasting love.

I don't want to be sacrilegious, but I wonder sometimes if the Godhead wouldn't be within rights to hold a "roast-the-parishioner" session between noon and one o'clock on Sundays.

Imagine what might be said about some of us: "That Ralph is amazing! Sings a perfect tenor with his voice, but all the time his mind is on the golf course."

"Yes, Susan was there, all fixed up as usual, but unfortunately, smart only on the outside. Inside she's worn that same spiritual smudge for months. I keep trying to tell her."

"Receiving money from Charlie is like being paid by a robot. It's a routine for which he's been programmed. Regardless of my needs, the amount never varies. What bothers me the most is his total lack of joy with his privilege of giving."

"I have a feeling the present traveling trophy for the Champion Late Arrivers should be retired. The Johnson family has such a lead now I don't think anyone will ever catch them. Sometimes I wish I weren't omniscient. It would be nice not to know everything!"

"What's it going to take to get through to young Norma? My convicting Spirit was practically shouting in her ear that she should get off this path she's been traveling, and she knows that I'm talking to her in this series of messages, but she just clams up!"

"It's really beginning to bother me that Larry's started to fall asleep again. I thought when the picture tube on his old TV blew out during the Saturday night late, late show, he'd take a hint and break that staying-up-late habit. Now the new color set *really* has him enamored and he's conking out again."

"What will I do, what will I do about these people at First Church? They go through the motions but nothing has meaning to them. You could take away any mention of my Son and never refer to my Holy Scriptures again, and they wouldn't even know the difference. It is just a religious routine with them."

Well, you get the idea, don't you? If someone habitually came to your house each week with the supposed purposes of showing you respect and of learning from you, but as time passed seemed never to accomplish either of these, what would *you* do?

On more than one occasion throughout history this was a problem for God as he saw the empty worship of his people. His thoughts on one such occasion were put into words by the prophet Isaiah as he began the Old Testament book that bears his name:

> "What to me is the multitude of your sacrifices?" says the Lord. "I have had enough of burnt offerings of rams and the fat of fed beasts; I do not delight in the blood of bulls, or of lambs, or of he-goats. When you come to appear before me, who requires of you this trampling of my courts? Bring no more vain offerings; incense is an abomination to me. New moon and sabbath and the calling of assemblies—I cannot endure iniquity and solemn assembly. Your new moons and your appointed feasts my soul hates; they have become a burden to me. I am weary of bearing them. When you spread forth your hands, I will hide my eyes from you; even though you make many prayers, I will not listen" (Isa. 1:11-15).

Isaiah was saying, loud and clear, that going through the motions wasn't a profitable religious exercise. The idea wasn't his alone, the message had come from God!

My thoughts for this chapter fit into one concise sentence: *Wise worshipers consider how God re-*

sponds to their worship.

Discerning people know that corporate worship is not designed just to meet their own needs. It is also an occasion to honor God.

What the Lord says to the congregation when it assembles is important to them, but of equal importance is what the body says *to God*. These worshipers are rightly embarrassed if the proclamation of the Word is less than what it should be. But even the finest of preaching won't balance the scales if Christians are not also maturing in their ability to give to God corporate praise, thanksgiving, or confession. Limited to one set of vocal cords all week, they regard it a special thrill to join many voices singing together:

Praise to the Lord, the Almighty, the King of creation! O my soul, praise Him, for He is thy health and salvation! All ye who hear, now to His temple draw near; Join me in glad adoration!

Often wise worshipers delight in the litanies written over the centuries by outstanding believers who were able to put into language what so many felt but could hardly express. Choral anthems draw assent from their hearts: "Amen. Amen. Yes, God, what they are singing to you and of you, I also affirm as being true!"

Unfortunately, these expressions seem to be the missing half in much of our congregational worship throughout this land. As believers, we can't seem to stretch out of ourselves into the majesty of God. We have neglected the wise considerations of what might also please him.

When we come right down to it, that's actually the primary meaning of the word *worship*. We usually think of worship as whatever happens during our services: preaching, singing, Scripture reading, even announcements. But when the word *worship* is used in the Bible, it most often refers to adoration or praise. It's the people telling God about the worth they see in him, lauding his great name, applauding his mighty deeds, magnifying who he is.

When I ended ten years of ministry at a church in Chicago, the dear people planned a beautiful service of farewell. Some former members even traveled a considerable distance to attend. Why had they come so far? Certainly not because it was a program from which they would personally profit. Rather it was their way of saying, "Pastor, we want this evening to be special for you and your family!" Their presence and love touched me deeply.

There is a question wise worshipers must train themselves to consider, which captures this same sentiment. We need to learn to inquire, *"God, what can I do to make this coming Sunday morning a more satisfying experience for you?*

"Maybe I need to pay more attention to what I'm singing—even try to hear the choral selection from your perspective. Maybe I need to get to bed earlier the night before or enter your house with clean hands and a pure heart.

"God, what can I do to make this coming Sunday morning a more satisfying experience for you?

"I'll do my best to be pleasant to my children and spouse as we get ready. Sure I can! Just wait and see! We'll even attempt to get there early!

"God, what can I do to make this coming Sunday

morning a more satisfying experience for you?

"I'll review my giving, pray in a special way for our pastor, even check with the church office to see if there's any way I can help when we arrive.

"God, what can I do to make this coming Sunday morning a more satisfying experience for you?"

If one out of ten worshipers would learn to be wise and consider Sunday mornings from God's perspective, what a difference it would make to God! If you are one of that ten percent, the route to and from church this Sunday could be one of the best you've traveled for some time.

2

THE CHRISTIAN'S HYMNAL

May I ask you a question about last Sunday's church service? During the congregational singing was your mind somewhere else, even though you followed the words and melodies of the various hymns? This happens far more often than most of us are willing to admit. Well, I have a remedy to suggest, but first let me establish a proper setting for my topic.

The Bible has much to say about singing to and of the Lord. In the space of this book I can't even begin to do justice to the total, but here are some sample passages:

"Sing to the Lord a new song, his praise in the assembly of the faithful! . . . Let them praise his name with dancing, making melody to him with timbrel and lyre! . . . Let them sing for joy on their couches. Let the high praises of God be in their throats" (Ps. 149:1-6).

"Let the word of Christ dwell in you richly, teach and admonish one another in all wisdom, and sing psalms and hymns and spiritual songs with thankfulness in your hearts to God" (Col. 3:16).

Psalm 47 is particularly appropriate to the point I wish to emphasize. "For God is the king of all the earth; sing praises in a skillful psalm and with understanding" (v. 7, The Amplified Bible). That last phrase, "with understanding," brings to mind Paul's words in 1 Corinthians 14.

In that chapter, you recall, he's writing about speaking in tongues. In such a context, Paul makes this comment: "I will sing with my spirit—by the Holy Spirit that is within me; but I will sing (intelligently) with my mind and understanding also" (v. 15).

Let me put into a sentence my basic thought: *It is good to sing of God with understanding.*

Yet how often is this actually done? Granted as twentieth-century believers we inherit certain problems regarding this, not the least of which is having so many songs available we can't keep up with them all.

Most worshipers can't meditate ahead of time on the hymns, because they aren't aware of what's scheduled until they arrive. Some people I know have formed the habit of arriving five minutes early and familiarizing themselves with the words of each hymn listed in the bulletin or on the hymn board. These organized few are far more prepared to participate *with understanding.*

"But our church doesn't have the order of service in the bulletin!" someone protests. Probably the choices would be listed somewhere if those in charge realized parishioners were truly interested.

My next suggestion regarding singing of God with understanding might best take the form of a question: If you wanted to buy a book to help someone spiritually and this individual already had a Bible, what would your number two choice be? Perhaps you want to encourage a new believer in his walk with Christ. Would you purchase a concordance, a one-volume Bible dictionary or atlas, a paraphrase, a Bible survey, maybe? Well, you already suspect what I'd suggest, don't you? I feel the best purchase would be a hymnal.

It was no less than John Wesley who felt each believer should carry two books at all times—a Bible and a hymn book. Somehow his advice has been lost through the years.

We should get back to using our hymnals. I find great delight working my way through such a book, reading the hymns on both sides of a given page each day. Meaningful verses or phrases are underlined just as one might mark a Bible. I notice who wrote the words and when, and think of whether or not the message of the text has meaning for me. Often one of the pieces becomes sort of a musical theme for my day. Surprisingly, by reading this way, I discover the intended meaning of words I have often sung but never before really understood.

If my voice were a bit more pleasing I'd sing the tunes in addition to reading the text, but even I don't like the way I sound alone! (Joining in chorus, however, with several hundred other Christians is a different story.) And if I were one of those who could play the piano as I go through the hymnal, it would be even better yet.

Then, I always pay attention to whether the words are addressed to God, like "Great Is Thy Faithfulness," or if they are written more to be heard by others, such as "How firm a foundation, ye saints of the Lord,/Is laid for your faith in His excellent Word!" After all, it seems important to me that a person knows who is being addressed when singing. Sometimes the hymn is actually a personal reminder, a song to oneself: "Be still, my soul:/The Lord is on thy side;/Bear patiently the/ cross of grief or pain."

With most hymnals, it's easier to begin this practice in the middle of the book because the songs of testimony are usually located there. More difficult ones like those of praise or adoration are usually the beginning selections. It's kind of like saying to a beginner in Bible reading, "Don't start in Leviticus or Isaiah. Pick one of the Gospels or a short epistle like First John or Philippians." The last thing I want is for you to stop what I'm suggesting after only the first three or four days.

Some obvious values result from this habit. For instance, in a short while you should begin to develop an appreciation for the really good hymns. Some songs will become absolutely majestic to you, while you'll be surprised at discovering others you always thought you enjoyed are little more than a catchy tune. Overall, you'll find yourself a much better judge of what really has value.

Much like we develop appreciation for the various writers of Scripture, you should also begin to appreciate some of the well-known creators of hymns: Charles Wesley, Isaac Watts, Fannie Crosby, and John Newton, to name a few. Then, quite often, you'll be surprised at how quickly you note that one song was written by some great hero of the faith, such as John Bunyan, or by Charles Spurgeon, or Martin Luther.

Along with insights into personalities, you will learn

much about how the church related to history. Here's a crusader's hymn, a Negro spiritual, a translation from Clement of Alexandria of the second century, a song from the Civil War period, music from the mass meetings of D.L. Moody, and on and on.

Spending time in a hymnal will also keep you honed doctrinally. A good hymnbook will have titles about the Father, the Son, and Holy Spirit, the Scriptures, the church, prayer, dedication, sanctification, the home and family, comfort, trust, and almost every other spiritual topic imaginable. The balance is healthy.

Of course, a big plus is that over a period of time you will become intimately acquainted with the hymns that are used in your church. And if it is good to sing to God with understanding, you will be one who qualifies because of the small time invested each day over a period of years.

"Good!" your heart will respond when you see number 259 listed in the bulletin: "And can it be that I should gain . . . "

"That's one of my favorites," you'll say. "It's by Charles Wesley. I especially like verse four, which I've memorized: "'Long my imprisoned spirit lay, /Fast bound in sin and nature's night;/Thine eye diffused a quickening ray./I woke, the dungeon flamed with light;/My chains fell off, my heart was free;/I rose, went forth, and followed Thee./Amazing love! How can it be/That Thou, my God, shouldst die for me.'"

And here's number 56: "Man of Sorrows, what a name/For the son of God who came,/Ruined sinners to reclaim!/Hallelujah! what a Saviour!" It's by the hymn writer, Philip P. Bliss, and a favorite of many.

"To God Be the Glory, "Guide Me, O Thou Great Jehovah," "How Great Thou Art," "A Mighty Fortress Is Our God," "All Hail the Power of Jesus' Name"—all the great hymns become more and more yours because as you sing them you do so with comprehension and mastery. And that's exciting, is it not?

Oh, yes, which hymnal do you buy? Naturally, purchase whichever one is used in the church you attend.

Start the routine of carefully reading two pages a day until you have gone through the book at least a couple of times. Before too long, a song you have carefully read and studied will be announced for one of your services and then the pay-off begins: You will be well on your way to singing to God with understanding.

3

THE LORD'S SUPPER

"Daddy, when will I be big enough to eat those crackers at church like you do and drink from one of the little cups?"

The truth is, for six-year-old Jeremy it's going to be a while yet. But then maybe a lot of adults aren't always ready to participate in communion either. At least, if they're honest, they will admit that during such sacred moments their minds are often on a thousand other things. Are you ever guilty of such neglect?

But perhaps, you feel too conspicuous to allow the elements to pass without partaking. If you don't receive them, surely someone will notice and assume you've committed a gross sin. But then on the other hand, you're not satisfied that you'll give the bread and the cup the dignity they deserve.

I've chosen to use the term, the *Lord's Supper*, because it is the one that appears in the biblical text from which my thoughts are drawn—1 Corinthians 11.

As you possibly know, the Lord's Supper has roots that go back into the Old Testament Passover feast. Celebrated yearly, this day commemorated the final plague upon the Egyptians, when the firstborn throughout the land were slain. The death angel passed over all the Israelites who had sprinkled blood on the doorposts of their homes. Falling in the first month, Passover was a high point of the Jewish calender year. The observance lasted a full week and the special meal was eaten the first evening. Uncircumcized strangers were not allowed to participate.

It was a Passover meal that Christ ate with his disciples in the upper room on that last evening before his arrest and crucifixion. As you recall, after Judas left the room (consistent with the teaching that the Lord's table is only for believers) Jesus took two of the prescribed Old Testament elements of the feast and infused them with new meaning.

Matthew records the sacred event:

> Now as they were eating, Jesus took bread [which would have been the unleavened kind], and blessed, and broke it, and gave it to the disciples and said, take, eat; this is my body." And he took a cup [this would have been one of three goblets of wine used in the Passover meal], and when he had given thanks he gave it to them, saying, "Drink of it, all of you; for this is my blood of the covenant, which is poured out for many for the forgiveness of sins (26:26-28).

So the old, the Passover, was incorporated into the new, our Lord's Supper, on this eve of deliverance from a tyrant worse than Pharaoh.

There is a certain mystery surrounding Christ's sayings, and there are differences of opinion as to precisely what he meant. Was he speaking literally or in a figure of speech?

Those holding to a sacramental view say that, when rightly observed, the bread and wine literally become the Body and Blood of Christ. Others give symbolic interpretation: they remain bread and wine but represent the broken body and shed blood of our Lord.

Those holding to a sacramental position must guard against drifting into magic and using the Lord's Supper as a good luck charm. There was a story in the Middle Ages about one woman who kept the bread in her mouth. When she reached home, she put it in her beehive, hoping for more honey. The bees, they said, built an entire cathedral in honeycomb! Obviously, such stories are an extreme to be avoided.

Those leaning to the symbolic side, must also be warned against a careless or casual observance. I have heard about a youth group having communion in a living room and using coke and potato chips. Now, that scares me too!

Apparently problems in connection with the Lord's Supper are not new. In our chosen passage, 1 Corinthians 11, Paul reproved his readers for their actions at the Table of Christ. He names greediness, contention, drunkenness, and humiliation of the poor. "Shall I commend you in this?" he asks. He answers, "No, I will not" (v.22).

What follows next are well-known words:

For I received from the Lord what I also delivered to

you, that the Lord Jesus on the night when he was betrayed took bread, and when he had given thanks, he broke it, and said, "This is my body which is for you. Do this in remembrance of me." In the same way also the cup, after supper, saying, "This cup is the new covenant in my blood. . . ."

Whoever, therefore, eats the bread or drinks the cup of the Lord in an unworthy manner will be guilty of profaning the body and blood of the Lord. Let a man examine himself, and so eat of the bread and drink of the cup. For any one who eats and drinks without discerning the body eats and drinks judgment upon himself. That is why many of you are weak and ill, and some have died" (vv. 23-30).

Paul's great concern, then, was that these people would act in a manner worthy of Christ's body and blood. That is the thrust of my remarks. *Christians should participate in the Lord's Supper in a manner worthy of Christ's body and blood.*

This statement doesn't pretend to solve the sacrament/symbol problem. It merely states again that Christians should participate in the Lord's Supper in a manner worthy of Christ's body and blood. But how do we do that?

See if these four questions help. Think of them during the Communion service. Better yet, review them quietly at home before you go to church.

Question 1: *Why has my King chosen these two elements to make his presence known?*

My question puts this celebration in the setting of royalty. My reason for doing this is twofold. First, while concentrating on the cross, it's easy to forget that the man crucified was actually the titled heir of the universe, the rightful sovereign who reigns over all creation. Second, such a picture underscores the honor and privilege that is ours of sitting at his great table. The very highest of nobility invites me to sit with him in his banquet hall.

But why has my King chosen these two elements to make his presence known—broken bread and a cup of wine. Do they reveal anything to me about him? "Share in them," he said, "in remembrance of me." How can these specific items help to bring to mind what Christ was like?

Question 2: *Have I possibly been disloyal since I last sat at my Lord's table?* The subject who fraternizes with the enemy has committed a serious offense in the sight of a warring king. He's upset, and rightly so, when he hears that a member of his kingdom has some kind of association with the enemy.

"Examine yourself," writes Paul. And that is reason enough for this kind of question: Have I possibly been disloyal since last sittting at my Lord's table? If your answer is yes, confession is in order.

Question 3: *Have I honored my monarch's command to love my fellow kingdom members?* That means the people sharing the bread and wine with you—do you love them? On the night of the Last Supper, John records Christ saying, three distinct times, "A new commandment I give to you, that you love one another." I think Christ would repeat the same thing were he to appear again: "By this all men will know that you are my disciples, if you have love for one another" (John 13:35).

"As I have loved you—"that's how Jesus said the Eleven ought to love each other. That's why I suggest you ask yourself, "Have I honored my monarch's command to love my fellow kingdom members?"

Question 4: *Am I ready for Christ's momentary return in splendor?* Paul writes, "As often as you eat this bread and drink the cup, you proclaim the Lord's death until he comes." Imagine that in the next Communion service the Son of God appears in all his glory. How would you respond? Would your heart rejoice? Could there possibly be mixed feelings on your part, sad ones as well as glad? Well, Jesus is coming again, you know, and he told us to live in such a way that we would be prepared at all times for that great event. So, ask yourself, "Am I ready for Christ's momentary return in splendor?"

These four questions are intended to help you participate in the Lord's Supper in a manner worthy of Christ's body and blood. If you take fifteen minutes to meditate on them in quiet on Saturday night, or early Sunday morning, I believe you'll enter the sanctuary with a sense of beautiful expectancy. Maybe you can keep the list in your Bible, and as the elements are being distributed, ask yourself these four questions. I believe you'll be able to focus your mind on the true meaning of the ceremony. At least, that's my hope.

Let's anticipate that soon we will experience the joy of the words to the song,

Welcome, all you noble saints of old,
As now before your very eyes unfold,
the wonders all so long ago foretold,

God and man at table are sat down,
God and man at table are sat down.
Elders, martyrs all are falling down,
Prophets, patriarchs are gathering round,
What angels longed to see now has been found,
God and man at table are sat down,
God and man at table are sat down.
Who is this who spreads the victory feast?
Who is this who makes our warring cease?
Jesus risen Savior, Prince of peace.
God and man at table are sat down,
God and man at table are sat down.

4

SQUARE PEGS IN ROUND HOLES

"Your qualifications are excellent! Unfortunately, they're not the ones needed for the job we're attempting to fill!" These words are probably spoken thousands of times every working day.

I believe that if God's people could learn the merit of evaluating people in the same way, they might find far greater enjoyment in their church. Numerous congregations are plagued with the square-peg-in-a-round-hole syndrome when it comes to their elected officers.

Imagine that you are a member of a church nominating committee. On what basis will you choose the names you eventually submit? Because the church is small and workers are few, do you resignedly hunt for anyone willing, though reluctant? Should you attempt to lobby for personal friends?

When you exercise the privilege of voting in a business meeting, do you put your check by the names of those most likely to maintain the status quo? Perhaps a candidate has a strong personality. Is that a good or bad sign?

What if you think you, yourself, should be considered for an office. Is it solely because you have proven your leadership skills in the business world? Or does being well-liked warrant the support of the rest of the congregation?

Many Christian organizations fill their executive boards with individuals who represent success in the marketplace. How do you respond to that practice?

Some religious organizations do not consider certain people for leadership roles because they are too young, or nonwhite or female.

In a sentence, the simple thought I want to underscore is: *When considering people for leadership positions in Christ's church, spiritual qualifications should be emphasized.* I know that doesn't sound overwhelmingly profound, but I believe it to be a truth of great importance.

Let me support the statement biblically, so you won't think it originated with me. Paul, writing in the first of his two letters to Timothy (chap. 3), states, "If anyone aspires to the office of bishop (or elder, or overseer—the words are interchangeable), he desires a noble task." And the verses that follow lend some beginning insights to the prerequisites Paul had in mind. I say "beginning insights" because certain specifics are included that today may seem almost ludicrous to write when compiling a list of qualified candidates.

For example, in verse 3 Paul tells Timothy the chosen person should not be a drunkard nor violent (more literally "a striker or hitter"). Now you have to admit it's a little funny to imagine reading minutes of your church board only to discover that Waldo Winebibber didn't vote because he was under the table all evening—stone drunk! Or, at precisely 3:37 P.M. the meeting was stopped because Percy Proudfist socked the moderator right in the teeth. You see, this list was constructed for a day when churches were being formed by converts won out of pagan surroundings. This fact may also account for the stipulation "husband of *one* wife," which sounds odd in our monogamous culture. Here's what Paul wrote:

> The saying is sure: If any one aspires to the office of bishop, he desires a noble task. Now a bishop must be above reproach, the husband of one wife, temperate, sensible, dignified, hospitable, an apt teacher, no drunkard, not violent but gentle, not quarrelsome, and no lover of money. He must manage his own household well, keeping his children submissive and respectful in every way; for if a man does not know how to manage his own household, how can he care for God's church? He must not be a recent convert, or he may be puffed up with conceit and fall into the condemnation of the devil; moreover he must be well thought of by outsiders, or he may fall into reproach and the snare of the devil" (1 Tim. 3:1-7).

So Paul believes that church leaders should be "above reproach." That certainly sounds like an overly strict requirement. Who is above reproach! The phrase literally means "those who cannot be laid hold upon" or "against whom there is no ground for accusation."

It's not perfection the apostle's expecting, but the phrase does imply that when a candidate is recommended he or she should be recognized by the congregation as a person against whom no charges could be made. If a person is elected to church leadership who is not spiritually qualified, the mistake will be costly in the long run. Choose those "above reproach."

The person should also be "temperate." A temperate climate is one that's neither too hot nor too cold. So a temperate church person is not an extremist, fixing on one point or facet of ministry, but unable to identify with the whole. Individuals who can only get excited about their own interests are probably poor choices for positions of overall leadership.

"Hospitable." This means someone whose home is regularly open to care for the needs of others, not just for entertaining friends. A good clue as to whether or not a person should be elevated to leadership in the body is the way the home is used.

"An apt teacher" (*apt* means qualified). Does the person know the Scriptures? That seems basic, yet I'm convinced there are far too many leaders making major decisions on church issues who have little more than a surface knowledge of the Word. According to Paul, the one in a position of responsibility should "hold firm to the sure word as taught, so that he may be able to give instruction [and encouragement] in sound doctrine and also to confute those who contradict it" (Titus 1:9).

"Gentle, not quarrelsome." A quarrel is a dispute

marked by anger, and believe me, that's the last thing needed when church leaders try to discern the mind of Christ. The overly opinionated entrepreneur may be great in business, but in the church? I agree with Paul that church leaders should be gentle people. I didn't say weak people, but gentle ones. That word in the Greek is the picture of a powerful animal that's been tamed. Gentleness is strength, strength that's been brought under proper control.

The right church leader "must manage his own household well, keeping his children submissive and respectful in every way." How practical the Scriptures are! In a church I served for ten years, the nominating committee would interview not only the candidate, but the spouse as well. The examining was always done in a spirit of love, but a party having marital problems or difficulty with children was protected from the heavy burdens of church leadership. The number one priority in such a case should be the creation of a healthy family. When the home area is strong, there will always be time for further service in the body. But I think it's unfair to request someone to spend hours concentrating on major matters of the church family if his own family is in need!

I haven't space to cover such qualifications as being sensible, dignified, not a recent convert, not a lover of money, well thought of by outsiders, although these are all included in 1 Timothy 3. But study this passage, or Titus 1:5-9, and remember: Paul is underscoring a basic principle: *when considering people for leadership positions in Christ's church, spiritual qualifications should be emphasized.*

I challenge you to compile a list of ten essentials you see as keys to spiritual maturity. Putting these biblical passages aside for a moment, write out a list of ten qualities you feel should mark all strong Christians.

For example, I would include a consistent prayer life. That's not been mentioned so far, but show me a person who has no time for prayer, and I'll point out someone who's not very close to the Lord. A second requirement would be someone who spends time in God's Word. Paul covers that one. Remember?

Sensitivity to the Holy Spirit's use of one's conscience is another area I see as important, as well as an awareness of spiritual warfare. A mindset that battles to overcome temptation and is concerned as to how the Kingdom fares in its war against the enemy—that's a quality I'd look for. The spirit of love is another essential ingredient, whether it's having compassion for the poor, playing the role of peacemaker, performing acts of kindness, or being gracious to children.

I'm halfway through my individualized list already, and what I'm doing is the same thing Paul did for Timothy. I'm suggesting you do it as well. Sit down and figure out what you see as ten key marks of spiritual maturing. What the exercise will accomplish is to fix in your mind the qualities you view as important.

When you're finished, compare your list with what Paul wrote to Timothy and Titus. Even his two lists aren't identical. There's overlap, but the specifics of 1 Timothy 3 and Titus 1 are not exactly the same. This only means the principle remains even though the details may differ.

In Acts 6, the twelve apostles told the Jerusalem

Christians to pick extra leaders who were "men of good report, full of the Spirit and of wisdom" (v. 3).

Certainly Scripture will take precedence over our personal lists. But the benefit of this exercise is to help you nail down the key qualities you'll be looking for the next time you're appointed to choose leaders in your church.

Finally, I'm concerned that the tone of this chapter not be too casual. There's a tremendous need for churches to be in the hands of praying, sensitive, mature Christian people. Obviously, to be spiritual doesn't mean one has to be poor or ignorant in business matters. But if for some reason such secondary skills are lacking, there's no reason why truly spiritual leaders can't confer with experts when consultation is needed.

Above all else, the church has to remain a spiritual body. Here is where the accent must rest. And oh! the pain that would be avoided if it did.

5

CHURCH LEADERS
EVERYONE LIKES

The seventh and last of the Narnia tales by C.S. Lewis is
entitled *The Last Battle* (Macmillan, 1970). Throughout the series the Christ figure is Aslan, a magnificent
lion who is greatly revered but seldom seen. As this final
book opens, it has been years since any of the creatures
in Narnia have laid eyes upon Aslan.

Now Shift, a wicked but clever ape, has found a lion
skin. He put it on Puzzle, a donkey, and spreads the
news that Aslan has returned. Because everyone's
memory of the lion is held so dear, none of the animals
dare fail to give him his proper respect. Yet, the way he
acts is strange. First, he only allows himself to be seen at
night, when it's quite dark, and second, all of his
messages are channeled through Shift, the ape.

Let me quote directly from Lewis:

"Now attend to me," said the ape with a nasty look. "I
want—I mean, Aslan wants—some more nuts. Those

you've brought aren't anything near enough. You must bring some more, do you hear? Twice as many and they got to be here by sunset tomorrow, and there mustn't be any bad ones or any small ones among them."

A murmur of dismay ran through the other squirrels, and the Head Squirrel plucked up courage to say:

"Please, would Aslan himself speak to us about it? If we might be allowed to see him—"

"Well, you won't," said the Ape. "He may be very kind (though it's a lot more than most of you deserve) and come out for a few minutes tonight. Then you can all have a look at him. But he will *not* have you all crowding round pestering him with questions. Anything you want to say to him will be passed on through me: if I think it's worth bothering him about. In the meantime, all you squirrels had better go and see about the nuts. And make sure they are here by tomorrow evening or, my word! you'll catch it" (pp. 27-28).

As you read, the charade is so obvious you wonder why the forest creatures didn't throw Shift out. But then why are so many supposed leaders allowed to misrepresent Christ on earth today?

The subject I have in mind for this chapter is the style of leadership practiced by those who represent our Lord. Have you ever observed "higher-ups" in the church, clergy or laity, and been impressed by the way they acted? Maybe your feelings were just the opposite! Is it possible that you hold a position of influence in a congregation? Do you have hopes of someday doing so? Are you ever in the role of choosing or voting for people who will occupy that kind of spot? And would you be at all curious as to whether Jesus' style of leadership was similar to the way church officials operate their churches today?

Most people would agree with my conviction that Christ is the greatest leader history has ever known. If you don't put him at the pinnacle, at the least you have to admit he was a most outstanding individual. Consequently, I propose examining what he said on this subject of leadership. If you're acquainted with Scripture, you're probably aware that his ideas ran counter to what most religious officials of his day thought, taught, or practiced.

Even his disciples (who had never really known firsthand the status, power, or wealth that often go with the top positions) were hard put to eliminate prevailing expectations from their minds. Matthew 20 is a good illustration of this. After three years of seeing her sons follow Jesus, the mother of James and John asked if they could sit on the master's right and left when his kingdom was ushered in.

The Scripture reads:

> When the ten heard it, they were indignant at the two brothers. But Jesus called them to him and said, "You know that the rulers of the gentiles lord it over them, and their great men exercise authority over them. It shall not be so among you; but whoever would be great among you must be your servant, and whoever would be first among you must be your slave; even as the Son of man came not to be served but to serve, and to give his life as a ransom for many" (vv. 24-28).

The same statement made today might sound this way: "You understand the manner in which secular leaders make clear to everyone who is in charge?

Without being told, even the most uninformed person would be able to pick out the boss. Why? Because the great ones openly exercise their authority over others. Those who identify with me, however, should not act like Shift the ape. Be servants. Place the well-bing of others above your own desires even as I demonstrated throughout my life. Leaders in my cause must be servants."

When I was pastor in Chicago, a Chinese-Filipino served with me for about five years. I'll never forget a story he told of his first day in Bible school. He came from a well-to-do home and was accustomed to the presence of servants. Upon conversion he chose to attend a small Chinese school to study the Scriptures. Upon arriving in the dorm he found the bathroom dirty so he reported the matter to the headmaster. Then my friend returned to his room to wait until someone was assigned this unpleasant duty.

Almost immediately he heard footsteps. As he looked out his door he was shocked to see the very man to whom he had just spoken. The principal, with bucket and rags, was on his way to personally take care of the task. After a few minutes of swishing and scrubbing, the leader came to his student's door and kindly reported that the washroom was now clean. My friend testified to having learned a great deal that day about servant-leadership.

This story is unusual, but too few leaders today have learned how compelling such an example is. They demand special recognition, devise various means of obtaining leverage, love to sit in the positions of greatest public exposure, and endlesssly tell who they are or they have done? "If you've got it, flaunt it!" says the world. Boast! Show off! To paraphrase a folk song:

Where have all the servants gone, long time passing?
Where have all the servants gone, long time ago?
Where have all the servants gone? Gone to strutting
  every one!
When will they ever learn? When will they ever learn?

"But, David, do you really believe a church leader—a pastor or board chairman or Sunday school superintendent—can be a servant and still get people to follow?"

Actually, that's not a new problem. Jesus often allowed people the option of leaving. If they marched to his drumbeat it was because they chose to, not because he forced them. And there were casualties—probably more than there were serious disciples. But know this: the true company of Christ stood out as a unique people in contrast to the world. His early leaders were known by all as those who served.

Would you like to play a key role among those perceived as God's present, peculiar people? Are you one who identifies with the name of Jesus but needs to be willing to practice his leadership style? After all this time could you relearn his basic lesson on this important topic?

Here it is! *Leaders in Christ's cause should practice being servants.* Radical? Yes! But does this style ever make the church more attractive!

A simple suggestion as to how to begin would be to memorize a verse found in Paul's second letter to the church at Corinth. In 2 Corinthians 4 are these words:

"For what we preach is not ourselves, but Jesus Christ as Lord, with ourselves as your servants for Jesus' sake" (v. 5).

That says it pretty well, doesn't it? You can make this verse your own by committing it to memory. Don't be content just to master the words. As you learn it, ask yourself, "What does this mean to me?"

Leaders in Christ's cause should practice being servants. It won't be easy. Many times bad habits have to be broken before good ones can be established.

The person who for years has batted cross-handed, or has always read with her finger tracing every word, or drives with a foot on the brake, has taken thirty minutes to deliver a sermon and now must learn to say everything in twelve—these must not expect to excel overnight.

But practice . . . train . . . exercise to think through what you're learning and work on enfleshing it. "Myself your *servant* for Jesus' sake. *Myself* your servant for Jesus' sake. Myself you servant for *Jesus'* sake." The effort is worth the strain.

Oh, for a church of servant'leaders across this land today!

6

CHURCHES THAT THRIVE

"What do you think is wrong with our church, Reverend Mains?" some out-of-town friends asked me the other day. "You've visited us and seen the potential," they continued. "Why, we have some of the finest people in all the world, and they're sincere in their desire to serve the Lord. But somehow we never seem able to put it all together. And the last couple of years attendance has dropped and enthusiasm has waned. What's the problem?"

Well, it's risky to give advice from a distance, but listening to their comments and drawing upon what I knew of the situation, their story reminded me of ancient Israel's wanderings in the wilderness. The shortest distance between two points is a straight line, but that generation of Jews apparently felt their meandering could get them to their destination just as well as God's prescribed route. Like a foolish runner looking for a shortcut in a hundred yard dash, they would eventually come to their senses. Almost forty years in the hostile Sinai Peninsula would see to that.

Whether this church, however, had experienced rocks and sand, wind and sun enough to admit they had gotten off course was another matter. Usually it takes people a long time to even agree that something is wrong. But evidence was beginning to mount. There was no momentum; service to God had been sucked of its joy and degenerated into oughtness. There were few converts. They were confused as to their direction. The accomplishment of even small tasks was far more difficult than what should be expected. There were frequent personality conflicts, repeated financial crises, hurt feelings, a shortage of workers, no keen sense of the Spirit at work in the services, staff workers leaving, long, difficult business meetings.

"Why, David," someone interrupts, "It's our church these people were talking about. Who was it that came to see you? I'll bet it was those blabbermouth . . ."

Stop! Hold on now! Sad to say, a lot of churches fit this description. But if your suspicions are aroused, perhaps you, too, will be interested in my response.

My observance of thriving churches has taught me that a common factor in congregations where the Spirit is alive, is the willingness of the people to follow godly leaders. Conversely, one key factor in withering local bodies, far more often than not, is the refusal of the people to be truly supportive of godly leaders. Was this not, in fact, the case with Israel under Moses?

The Book of Numbers tells of the departure from Mount Sinai. In less than three weeks this man of God remarkably organized 600,000 far-from-perfect people, and in just another eleven days they had reached Kadesh-Barnea on the very threshold of the Promised Land. But here, as before in several critical ways, the people of Israel refused to fall in line with what Moses said should be done.

"But, David, already you're assuming our pastor is a Moses," someone says. "And that's just not the case. This one we've got should never have been fished out of the bulrushes!"

Would you mind if I addressed myself in the next chapter to men in the ministry who, for one reason or another, are less than what God expects of them? Right now, I want to concentrate on the need for believers to learn to follow godly leaders—not perfect ones, but godly. Do you see your minister as a man who sincerely purposes to honor Christ in his life, rather than someone who seems to hold his position for less honorable reasons? Do you feel the basic motivation of your pastor is that of ministering to you on Christ's behalf?

If your answer is yes, then my response is, regardless of whether your clergyman is brilliant or slow, entrancing or slightly dull, bold or shy, educated or degreeless, genteel or foot-in-the-mouth variety, traditional or contemporary—as a congregation, you'll get far more done for the Lord and be happier in the process (and feel better about your behavior when this man is eventually called elsewhere) if you can learn while he's with you to follow the direction he sets instead of fighting him at every turn.

If a panel of experts were to pick the best ideas

floating around in a given congregation, I presume they seldom would favor those of the minister. But if the same panel were asked which plan fits the personality of the person expected to give leadership, it obviously is going to be the minister's, because he thought of it!

And you know what? The truth is, there are any number of workable ways to accomplish a job if people are willing to cooperate. No plan, no matter how brilliant, works well if they won't. If something my minister proposes sounds reasonable, I'm going to support him, even if it's not necessarily the way I would have organized or administered a particular program. That's because there's not enough time in life to sulk over whether or not he's doing things my way. Oh, if certain people could only learn this!

"But, David, my problem is not over how something is done, but which ministries are chosen as important to begin with."

As far as I'm concerned, they are practically the same thing. It's not worth splitting a congregation over which is better—to use extra funds to start a church library or take on a new missionary. Either way the Lord will be honored. Why not discover what the pastor thinks? Maybe it doesn't matter to him. But if it does, what are the reasons for his feelings? Could you lay down your desires and support his?

"I'm beginning to react," you say. "You sound like you're proposing everyone should just roll over and play dead and let the preacher make all the decisions."

No, I'm not. And most ministers aren't that bull-headed. (Some, yes!) But when it comes to a church deciding on direction, the options are always multiple.

It's disheartening for a leader to pray and work and talk things over with others and then enthusiastically lay out what he believes to be the Lord's will, only to have it ground into oblivion because others don't realize that the reason they like another plan so much better is primarily because they thought of it. If a church continually imposes their preferences or plans on a pastor, he will in time become extremely uncomfortable directing a program his heart's not in and his personality doesn't fit.

I believe that churches fall into two categories in this regard. One is made up of people who wisely realize they will never get anywhere without an acknowledged leader. If their pastor is a godly man, they should make every effort possible to follow his guidance. The second group is expert at demonstrating how flawed men of God happen to be. And they're correct! Ministers are as human as the rest of mankind. But what does that prove?

Guess into which category the church of my out-of-town friends fits? Why, people of that congregation were notorious for frustrating preachers. From outright refusal to cooperate, to underground criticism, to stalls, to power plays, to hair-splitting, to misdirected anger against all authority figures, to asking proof that a proposal is what God wants—you name it, they did it! And now time had taken its toll.

What did they need? My prescription was that these people needed first to find a pastor they felt walked with God. Second, they should vow to cooperate with everything he suggested for one complete year, just to see if such a radical remedy would work. I think it would

. . . if the strain of adjustment didn't kill off a few in the process!

I believe *churches thrive that learn to follow godly leaders.* God's people wander in a wilderness when they refuse to put their confidence in the person commissioned to lead. The children of Israel finally returned to the threshold of Canaan. The same orders were issued and this time obeyed and the people took the land. But it was not the same generation, nor was it the same leader. Those who fought against Moses had all died, and he, too, was gone. The new opportunity was offered by Joshua to their children. It's sad, isn't it?

"Your remarks are way too onesided, David."

I know it. The next chapter addresses pastors, remember? Then they may feel somewhat the same way.

This is not a day for fooling around. There's too much at stake in this land and in the world. I speak strongly because I'm impatient with churches that have been at a virtual standstill for years just because they are devoted to the syndrome of too-many-chiefs-and-not-enough-Indians.

Yes. As a member of a local body I'll share my opinions and I'll even take a stand, when necessary, on a matter of doctrine or ethics. But I'm not going to pick up the sword against my pastor over areas of leadership that are mostly opinion or style. I can do things his way. When the territory is won and we're relaxing, then there'll be more than enough time to argue and fight. But right now, I'm more anxious to enter that good land. I for one am content to claim that victory the way a godly pastor proposes.

7

A WORD TO
MINISTERS

Here's a multiple choice question. Ready? Today's ministers are characterized by:

    a) a strong positive self-image and great enthusiasm.

    b) job frustration and average motivation.

    c) lack of urgency and feelings of insignificance.

I don't know how you would answer, but I see men in my profession all the time. In my opinion, they generally manifest a lack of urgency and have feelings of insignificance. Category (c) is most accurate.

To put it differently, not too many men of the cloth start their morning thinking, "What I have to do this day is of vital importance to my congregation, my community, my nation, my world." Rather, ministers tend to see themselves as having a lot of work to do, but also struggling with the difficult job of relating to people who aren't really convinced of a minister's importance. Maybe, like a cavalryman in the army, we're interesting to have around and great for ceremonial effects. But let's face it, the real world seems to have discarded horse soldiers and clergymen.

There are reasons for this insecurity. One, it's easy for us to be intimidated by society's attitudes. Preachers are communicators. But in this land our voices are very small compared with the incredible power of the secular media. Maybe I should explain that word. The secular world view rejects the relevance of religious faith.

Not that morality is completely eliminated; newspapers, magazines, radio, and tv stations still give editorials and opinions. It's just that spiritual conceptions are not the foundation of their views. Oh, religion can still be the source for a news item, an interview, or a documentary, but a continuing emphasis that reflects God's thought is not welcome. In fact, the opposite is true.

Possibly, the freedoms on which our country was founded make this necessary. But present secular communications tend to subtly teach our people to view news events and national life as though God had little or nothing to do with them. Ministers have suffered greatly from their own inability to help people successfully integrate faith with this mix of everyday life.

I for one don't think a thirty-minute sermon once a week is enough to counteract all that the average Christian hears and sees and reads and absorbs from secular sources. It's a far different world than it was fifty years ago. I thank god for the great move of his people into broadcasting. I'm glad for religious books and magazines, recordings, and direct mail processes. In spite of some of the problems created, these things have been a stabilizing factor for many believers. Yet influences like this are still not nearly as effective as hoped. I feel we ministers are characterized as being unable to close the gap.

The next reason for insecurity among ministers is that there has been an unfortunate tendency for preachers to see their gifts minimized within the church in the exciting process of encouraging others to develop theirs. Again and again, I've watched it happen.

Like juveniles becoming adult, who in the process sometimes need to put down their parents, congregations have often experienced spiritual growth in God's household at the minister's expense. Hear me now. Recognizing the need for all members of the body to function, we must also clearly establish that certain gifts still remain more important than others. The ones at the top of the scriptural lists relate to the wise handling of the Word.

Too many times recently I have been aware of an attitude emerging that insinuates the minister really isn't that important. "Why, we can preach and teach also. Listen to us." I'm glad such gifts are being expressed, but there's a vast difference between filling the pulpit on occasion and shepherding a flock through good and bad because of a divine commission that will eventually require an accounting before God himself. In the past I've been guilty, while helping laity understand the importance of their gifts, of failing to emphasize the greater importance of the minister's appointed authority and exposition of Scripture. But never again!

Third, many preachers have lost their sense of significance because failures within their profession have become intimidating to all. It's difficult to produce a man of God through education, the way a doctor or a lawyer is trained. There are standards, but a degree doesn't indicate competence in ministry nearly as much as it might in other fields. Also, there is always the need to remain open to the fact that the Lord may anoint a world changer who's studied very little in seminary—like a D.L. Moody or Billy Sunday. Charles Finney was trained as a lawyer, not a preacher, but God wanted him, too.

Unfortunately sometimes allowing for exceptions can lead to abuses. We see this when a Rev. Jim Jones in Guyana becomes the major news story of the year.

Even with ordination behind us and possessing a good reputation, ministers are often ashamed of how incompetent we feel in representing God. Outstanding successes (thank the Lord for them) are still usually fewer than efforts that end up in mediocrity. This pain is shared by all but the most insensitive among our ranks.

These factors, as well as others, have had a major bearing on who we ministers are and how we act.

In spite of these negative insecurities, let me balance the scales by sharing some verses from God's Word.

Now when I went to Troas to preach the gospel of Christ and found that the Lord had opened a door for me, I still had no peace of mind, because I did not find my brother Titus there. . . .

But thanks be to God, who always leads us in triumphal procession in Christ and through us spreads everywhere the fragrance of the knowledge of him. For we are to God the aroma of Christ among those who are being saved and those who are perishing. To the one we are the smell of death; to the other, the fragrance of life. And who is equal to such a task? Unlike so many, we do not peddle the Word of God for profit. On the contrary, in Christ we speak before God with sincerity, like men sent from God (2 Cor. 2:12-17, NIV).

That's the preacher Paul writing. He started his day, I'm sure, convinced the job he was doing was important. Here was a man certain that there could be no greater calling. His work was as important to him as life and death itself. He was a minister who couldn't imagine a profession more vital than to reveal God's words to the world.

Somehow, I sense Paul would write to us as fellow ministers, "Always in my heart is a prayer that you who share my calling understand how critical a role we play. For if you men are not strong, the cause suffers dramatically. If you who communicate God's thoughts speak lifeless words, whence will come the fire?"

You know what I think? *Today's ministers need to regain a sense of their extreme importance.*

We need, you and I, fellow preachers, a breakthrough in terms of how we view ourselves. God help us to once again be captured by our calling. Let us strive together to again become driven men, aware that what we have been divinely entrusted to spread by our lives is the very aroma of Christ himself—a putrid smell of death to some but the delightful fragrance of life to others. Can such urgency be aroused in this generation of proclaimers?

"Why, thank you, David. A little pep talk is nice now and again."

No, no, my brother, the problem is far bigger than can be helped by a hyped-up locker room challenge. People today stand in desperate need of a word from God. But the clergy are not responding to the challenge. What factors have combined to make us more careful, more casual, more cheerful than God's messengers should really be?

The fault, no matter the cause, is one only we can change. Can the image of ourselves be altered in our own heads from necessary to vital, from periphery to strategic, from optional to mandatory? Mere words can't bring about the metamorphosis, but the message burns in my heart that ministers must be challenged to a fresh awareness of how vital they are at this moment in time.

As a start, I am asking God to somehow imbue afresh in me a deep awareness of the smell of death, and the fragrance of life that supernaturally marks me as I go about my tasks.

God, don't let me be a mere peddler of your Word. May I work and pray and study and preach as "a man sent from God."

Only from such fresh commitment on your part as well, my fellow minister, can this land be preserved.

8

INTRODUCING CHANGE IN A TRADITIONAL CHURCH

Guess what question I have been asked most frequently in my ministry? Probably only a handful of you will know. Yet the same inquiry has come up again and again. Because of the years I spent in Chicago pastoring in what many refer to as a renewal church, time and again someone will still ask, "David, if you were to take a traditional pastorate, how would you bring such a congregation into line with renewal principles?"

Because most of my pastoral work took place in the freedom of a church that I founded, I presume many feel the transference of certain important principles to the life of a more typical setting would be automatically ill-fated. This isn't necessarily true.

What advice would I give to the person who, though still belonging to the First Traditional Church, is quite anxious to introduce change? Or to the man with new ideas who has just been called to such a setting as pastor?

First, I would check to make sure I was personally experiencing the kind of Christianity I hoped to introduce.

It's important that you have a sense of well-being regarding your current spiritual condition before you attempt to help someone else. I recall one very bitter minister who was almost obsessed with the need for new life in the church. But he personally manifested the very characteristics that needed to be eliminated in order for God's Spirit to move. In fact, his leadership was like the kiss of death wherever he went.

Having witnessed this same syndrome more than once, I now view such a person (short-tempered, critical, bitter, touchy, casting himself in the role of a salesman of spiritual refreshment) as a little like a child-hating, ill-mannered grouch applying to peddle ice cream bars for the Good Humor Company!

Because someone read a book about a church that experienced new life doesn't qualify him or her to be the channel through which it can be infused into their local setting. To admire another who made it work doesn't mean you are automatically qualified to duplicate the role of church-mover.

If there is anything for which renewal stands, I suppose it would be a basic honesty. If a renaissance is not at work in your own life, be honest enough not to seek to promote it among others. According to Scripture, true evidences that God is working in you should include a love for people, an inner joy, peace, patience, self-control, and kindness. I also believe renewal people experience continuing fellowship with God because of having matured in both prayer and the appreciation of his Word.

Rejuvenated believers aren't perfect, but they certainly are improving in their ability to overcome temptation! The fact that such growth is taking place in you should be obvious to everyone. This is the key factor that will determine the degree to which others are willing to follow your suggestions.

Granted, renewal in a church fosters personal growth. But to think the eventual corporate experience will make up for a present personal lack is wishful thinking. In fact, congregational renewal characteristically involves a great amount of pain as well as joy. It therefore should be overseen by the spiritually mature, not by fledglings.

The second prerequisite for renewal is to capture the people with a vision of what the New Testament church was like.

I'm convinced the average Sunday church attendant has a poor understanding of God's magnificent intentions regarding his body. It's quite possible that most parishioners feel satisfied with nothing more than steady growth in attendance, donations, and community influence. Unfortunately, money, prestige, or size don't guarantee the presence of the Lord.

Ultimately, the church should be viewed as a model of *society as intended by God.* Here believers, under the tutoring of the Holy Spirit, are being matured in their love for the Lord and their regard for fellow humans. In a culture of alienated people, the church should therefore be able to say, "If you're looking for acceptance, you'll be sure to find it here!"

"We care and want to be of help," it assures casta-ways. "Your search for justice and mercy ends with the people of God," it cries out to the dehumanized. In the midst of confusion, the fellowship of Christ sounds a clear note regarding forgiveness, truth, and peace, and displays that about which she speaks.

"Sounds idealistic!" you say.

Well, if this "idealistic" description is not true of a congregation, it's a sure sign that the Lord's presence is not being experienced the way he would like it to be. For were Jesus literally the leader in a given church, it should be demonstrating for all to see the matchless ability of our Lord to refashion not only individuals but groups, or societies as well. Is this not exactly what we observe in the Book of Acts?

Churches like this still exist. In fact, recently I preached in one! Now I know the minister much better than I do the congregation, but without question the members there have assimilated this man's vision of their church as intended by the Lord. To be even superficially involved, as I was, is to share in the joy and excitement and outreach of Christ at work today through this manifestation of his body. Without a vision the people perish.

Here is the third point of advice I would give a person who wanted to introduce change in a lifeless setting: *Begin with less threatening areas. Encourage the congregation in the process of slow but steady growth.*

That last word, *growth,* was chosen purposely, and I would advise making a conscious effort to talk about growth rather than change. Most people don't like to change, but they are open to growing! Note that this adjustment in vocabulary is not an effort to be deceptive, for growth is another of those words that parallels renewal.

Growth also suggests slow but steady progress.

"How many years will it be before my people learn to truly love each other?" is a realistic question. It will take a while—years, in most instances. Visions can be understood quickly. Seeing them realized doesn't occur quite as fast.

The church to which I referred earlier has been in this growth process under their pastor's leadership for over fifteen years. He has refused many opportunities to minister elsewhere because of a commitment to see God's desires fulfilled in that place. Woe to the reformers who will "give it six months but if things haven't turned around by then I'm leaving!"

In my mind, three key characteristics will be present if a church becomes the present visible manifestation of Christ in the world. One: There will be love among the believers. Two: A congregation will become proficient in prayer. And three: God will be able to minister through his body by means of the gifts of the Holy Spirit. These are the key areas to which I would devote most of my teaching in order to see desired growth. After all, we're in trouble if parts of the body are not working together in harmony, or if communication with the head has broken down, or if jobs are not accomplished because fingers or ears are insensitive to the importance of their immediate response to divine instructions.

Possibly the least threatening of these basic matters would be the topic of prayer. Too many churches split on matters that are wiser to back away from. Can we use a guitar in the sanctuary? Shall we serve coffee between services? Renewal and being different or contemporary aren't always synonymous. In fact, I have often found the traditional forms to be the most appropriate ones for conveying what is in mind.

I would begin by assisting my congregation to understand private praise, thanksgiving, confession, petition, intercession, expressing feelings, fasting, and so on. Then they would be taught how to put these same prayers into the corporate setting. "*We* attribute worth to you. *We* praise you, God." "*Together We* thank you." "Hear the feelings *we* express." "As a people *we* confess our shortcomings."

Over a period of time more difficult areas, such as the gifts of the Holy Spirit, could be introduced. But, always the renewal emphasis would be on how best to strengthen these three basic relationships: man to man, man to God, the gifts of the Holy Spirit in relationship to ministry.

Finally, *realizing the many difficulties involved in renewal, I would maintain an attitude of allowing the church the option of not following my leadership.*

There's a vital difference between God's ideal and the present status of American congregations. Though there is often agreement and much cheering as the journey begins between "what has always been" and "what the future holds," attitudes have a way of changing when the going gets harder.

This happened often in the ministry of Jesus himself. He knew what was coming. Yet he never forced people to follow him. Likewise, I would encourage all those who cherish new dreams for a given church to allow original members the privilege of saying "far enough" anywhere along the trail.

It's not your call to issue in God's desires against all obstacles. You are to lead until people no longer choose to follow. When that happens, and it often does, it's time to level off for a while or go elsewhere. The history and properties and associations were there before you came and should remain for others to contribute to after you leave.

Therefore a call to renewal, despite my insistence to give growth time, has a certain nomadic flavor to it. You live literally with "tent pegs in hand," always aware it may be time to pull up stakes. I'm not suggesting an "if-you-won't-play-my-way-I'll-take-my-marbles-and-go" attitude. Rather, it's the simple recognition that these rapids have claimed a rather large number of travelers, so be programmed for the possibility of being swamped yourself.

Now you have my answer to the question most frequently addressed to me. I just wish I could be assured of a positive response regarding the question I most frequently ask myself: In my lifetime will God allow me to witness another great day of his church?

9

TOO SOON TO QUIT

If you are one of God's servants who have been considering throwing in the towel, this chapter is geared to you.

It's not that you don't want to keep on or that you aren't walking with the Lord. It's just that right now you're tired of getting nowhere in terms of your assigned ministry. Perhaps you're a Sunday school teacher who has convinced yourself no one is paying any attention anymore. Maybe you are a missionary on furlough, wondering if it's really worthwhile to return for another term. Or you could be a church lay leader experiencing a little more than the normal traumas of being in spiritual leadership. Maybe you're in a faith ministry, and wonder if the needed support will ever come in. Are you a pastor who could give a thousand illustrations of what it's like to labor hard and get nowhere in God's service? At any rate, right now you've had it!

It's like fighting the new boy across the street when you were little. That was great fun until he got on top of you and wouldn't get off. It was too humiliating to give up—everyone was watching. But try as you would you couldn't throw him. Why, you'd swear he's been trained by Strangler Lewis! Now what do you do? It hurts to quit, and it hurts to continue—you're not sure which is worse! Though you go through the motions of struggle, all the onlookers know you've given up the fight.

Well, pay attention. What I'm going to say isn't shared very often, but it's true nevertheless. Your experience is a common one!

In fact, I doubt if there's been a significant breakthrough in the history of the church without a great struggle on someone's part. We've been led to believe that spiritual successes come quickly and easily if we just do the right things. But that isn't always true. Too often we've been guilty of underestimating the strength and cleverness of the enemy. How many times have his territorial claims been challenged without a battle royal resulting? Maybe one of the greatest weaknesses in the cause of Christ today is the tendency to give up too soon.

I think it would be helpful if more time could be spent studying the biographies of Christian servants. For example, the American missionary, David Brainerd, went through periods of extreme darkness. When asked, "What can be done in order to revive the work of God where it is decayed?" John Wesley replied, "Let every preacher read carefully the life of David Brainerd."

Brainerd's days were short, but the influence of his

devotion is still felt, moving others to a noble forgetting of self. Born in 1718 and early orphaned, he inherited a sickly body, which would succumb to bouts of tuberculosis. Trained at Yale, his first desire had been overseas missionary work. But soon his gaze focused on the needs of the Indians in his native land who had been miserably debased by the white man's vices and were despised as inferior creatures. Brainerd saw them as human beings deserving the message of Christ's love. Eagerly he accepted the appointment of the Scottish Society for Promoting Christian Knowledge to labor as our missionary among the Indians.

He had little success working by himself in what he called his most lonesome wilderness, where he slept on a heap of straw. The Indians were indifferent. Worse yet, they were suspicious of white men and they bitterly resented his presence. His health began to decline rapidly so that after a year of unremitting toil and hardship, he was forced to retire from the field.

Invited to pastor several New England churches, the temptation was very strong to settle in East Hampton. Here in a lovely country, amid wealthy, kindly people, he would be able to recover his strength and spend happy and useful days. Also, there was a romantic tie for him with a daughter of Jonathan Edwards. Did not his experience show that further work with the Indians would mean certain and possibly even a speedy death? Besides what fruit had he to show for his labors? Certainly an opportunity in East Hampton where health and love and service awaited him must be from God.

As Brainerd hesitated, it seemed that from the far-off woods came the pathetic wail of "his" people. His assignment among them was not yet completed. Literally taking his life in his hands, he set out again for the wigwams and the campfires.

His Journal from this point is a record of traveling back and forth through pathless forests, over mountain ranges, in fierce rains and freezing cold. His body was reduced to a pitiably weakened state. But as his strength ebbed it seemed his compassion grew, until his desire for God to work became a hunger that was not to be denied. Whole nights were spent alone in the woods in agonizing prayer, and the forces of God joined him in his battle as the Spirit seemed to be poured out upon Brainerd's region of the Susquehanna Valley.

Now it seemed Indians pressed upon him from all sides, grabbed hold of the bridle of his horse, desperate to hear God's way of salvation. Strong men who could bear the most acute torture without flinching could no longer conceal their pain as God's arrow pierced them through. In distress they cried out, "Lord, have mercy." Now as the frail, young missionary spoke, one by one hundreds came to peace in the comfort of the Gospel.

As time passed Brainerd had full proof that a heaven-sent revival had come—a passion for righteousness possessed the converts. Victims of the white man's firewater were delivered. Indian camps were cleansed from their physical and moral filthiness, and the love of Christ expelled every unlovely thing. A strong Indian church was established, some of their own becoming missionaries.

Brainerd's body, utterly exhausted by his labors, was quickly mastered now by disease. But what did that matter? It had endured until the divine purpose had its perfect fulfillment. When in 1747 he breathed his last, it's said that he died in an ecstasy of joy. He was twenty-nine years old.

Numerous other examples could be cited of men and women of God who remained steadfast in the face of adversity. The Apostle Paul wrote to the people of Corinth, "We do not want you to be ignorant, brethren, of the affliction we experienced in Asia; for we were so utterly, unbearably crushed that we despaired of life itself" (2 Cor. 1:8).

He also said:

Five times I have received at the hand of the Jews the forty lashes less one. Three times I have been beaten with rods; once I was stoned. Three times I have been shipwrecked; a night and a day I have been adrift at sea; on frequent journeys, in danger from rivers, danger from robbers, danger from my own people, danger from Gentiles, danger in the city, danger in the wilderness, danger at sea, danger from false brethren, in toil and hardship through many a sleepless night, in hunger and thirst, often without food, in cold and exposure. And, apart from other things, there is the daily pressure upon me of my anxiety for all the churches (2 Cor. 11:24-28).

Between these two sections is the fabulous sentence: "Therefore, having this ministry by the mercy of God, we do not lose heart" (2 Cor. 4:1). I like that very much, don't you? Especially when we consider the life of the one who said it. "We do not lose heart." A little later he adds, "We are afflicted in every way, but not crushed; perplexed, but not driven to despair; persecuted, but carrying in the body the death of Jesus, so that the life of not forsaken; struck down, but not destroyed; always Jesus may also be manifested in our bodies" (vv. 8-10).

That's the message I have for you. If God gave you your present position of service and up until now he has not said you should leave it, don't throw in the towel just yet. Don't quit until your Commander says to leave. Take heart even as you read.

My thrust sentence is: *People given assignments by God should not lose heart. Or stated positively,"People given assignments by God should remain steadfast in adversity.*

I was fortunate to be in Wheaton College under the presidency of Dr. V. Raymond Edman. Many of you, no doubt, have read some of his numerous books. He was truly a saint of a special kind whom I've come to appreciate more and more as I've grown older. Often he would speak on this topic to college students. "It's always too soon to quit," he would say. I still remember the words, the sound of his voice, and his addressing us as "brave sons and daughters true."

It's funny how a man's sermons can stick with you even after he's been gone for some time. I have a feeling that if Doc Edman could come back to life and share some words with you even today, he'd probably say the same thing, "Brave son, it's always too soon to quit! Daughter true, not somehow but triumphantly!"

So I would add also, my special friend, if you find yourself hurting while serving the greatest of all masters, don't let the situation get the best of you. Stand firm. Act in a way that will make Christ proud. Rejoice in him. Probably it's too soon to quit!